Contents

A **healthy** body

A healthy body helps you to stay well and happy.

Here are some ways to keep healthy.

Eating and drinking

Keeping
clean

Exercise

Sleep

Are you keeping healthy?

Our bodies work hard all the time. We need energy for everything we do. We get energy from food.

Rice

Bread

Potatoes

Pasta

Oats

These foods contain large amounts of energy.

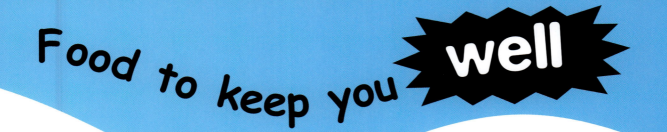

We need to eat different kinds of fruit and vegetables to keep well.

Which of these do you like to eat?

What vegetables are on this kebab?

9

Food to help you grow

Everyone grows at their own rate. These foods help people to grow.

Cheese

Lentils

Beans

Eggs

Meat

Fish

What do you eat to help you grow?

To stay healthy you need foods for energy, keeping well and growth. You also need plenty to drink.

Sam and Hannah want to make a healthy meal.

What could they choose? Turn the page to find out.

Sam has chosen chicken, rice and vegetables. This has food for growth, for energy and for keeping well.

Here is another healthy meal.

potato, cheese, salad

Hannah has chosen a beefburger and cheese. She has not chosen any foods for keeping well or for energy.

Here is another less healthy meal.

banana, potato

What should you always remember to do before you eat? Turn the page to find out.

You should wash your hands before eating. You should also wash them after going to the toilet.

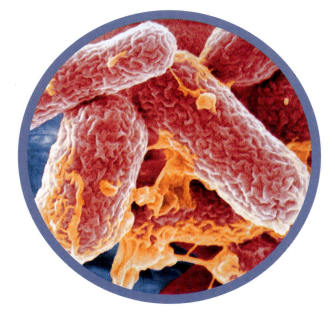

This is to wash away tiny living things called germs. You can only see germs through a powerful microscope!

Some germs can make you ill if they get into your body.

Paul, Katie and Nicole have dirty hands. They each wash them for 15 seconds.

Katie uses cold water.

Paul uses cold water and soap.

Nicole uses warm water and soap.

Who will have the cleanest hands?

Turn the page to find out.

Nicole has the cleanest hands.

Warm water and soap are best for washing your hands.

Remember to dry your hands after you have washed them.

16

The rest of your body needs a good wash too.

Your skin makes sweat to keep you cool. The sweat makes your skin dirty. Germs like to live in the dirt.

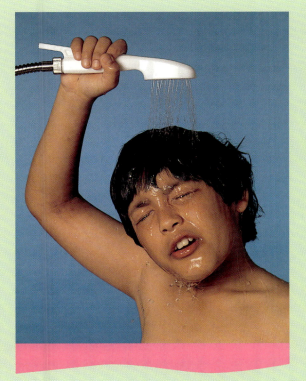

Wash your body every day to stop germs living on your skin.

What else should you clean every day? Turn the page to find out.

Teeth

You need to clean your teeth every day. This keeps them healthy so you can bite and chew your food.

We have two sets of teeth. We get our first set at about six months old - our milk teeth.

At about six years old we start to lose our milk teeth. Bigger, adult teeth take their place.

There are three ways to keep your teeth healthy.

1. Clean them in the morning and at night.

2. Try not to eat lots of sugary foods.

3. Visit the dentist twice a year.

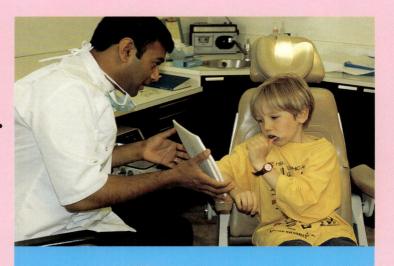

Exercise

Taking exercise also helps to keep your body healthy.

Exercise keeps your joints healthy.

Exercise makes your muscles stronger.

There are lots of ways to take exercise. These children are going to school.

Hannah is walking.

Alex is going in a car.

Who is taking the most exercise? Turn the page to find out.

Hannah is exercising her arms and legs by walking to school.

Tom

Sarah

Sophie

Which parts of the body are Tom, Sophie and Sarah exercising?

Taking a **rest**

Sam and Nicole have been playing outside for an hour.

Why do they need to sit down and have a drink and a snack?

23

Being **ill**

Sometimes you feel ill. You may feel hot or have aches. You may cough or sneeze or even be sick.

You may need to see a doctor.

Sometimes medicines can help you get better.

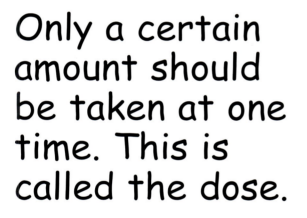

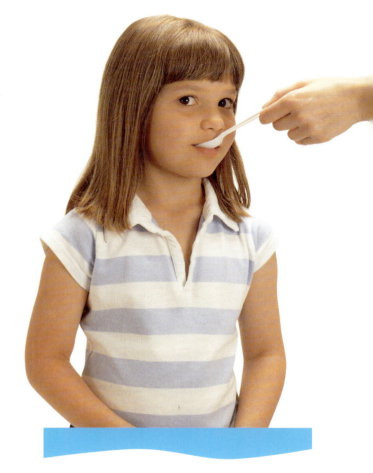

Only a certain amount should be taken at one time. This is called the dose.

It is important that a grown-up gives you your dose of medicine.

What else helps you to get better? Turn the page to find out.

Sleep

We need lots of sleep when we are ill – and to stay healthy.

When we sleep, our bodies rest. We have more energy.

If we do not get enough sleep we feel tired and grumpy.

If we get enough sleep we feel fit and lively.

How long do you sleep? Make a table like this and fill it in.

Day	Lights out	Wake up
Sunday		
Monday		
Tuesday		
Wednesday		
Thursday		
Friday		
Saturday		

Useful words

dentist – a person whose job is to look after teeth.

doctor – a person whose job is to try and make sick people get better.

dose – the correct amount of medicine that should be taken at one time.

energy – the power we get from food, which makes us able to be active, and keep warm.

exercise – to be active.

germs – tiny living things that can spread disease and make you feel ill. Germs are too small to see.

healthy – fit and well.

illness – something that makes you feel unwell.

joint – a point in the body where two bones fit together.

lentil – a kind of dried seed.

medicine – a liquid, tablet or spray that you take when you are ill.

microscope – a tool that makes it possible for us to see tiny things.

muscle – one of the parts inside the body that makes movement.

sweat – a liquid that comes out of your skin when your body is hot.

Some answers

Here are some answers to some of the questions we have asked in this book. Don't worry if you had some different answers to ours; you may be right, too. Talk through your answers with other people and see if you can explain why they are right.

Page 9
The vegetables on the kebab are onion, courgette, mushroom and pepper.

Page 10
You may not like all these foods but hopefully you like to eat some of them. There are many different ways to eat these things, for example eggs can be scrambled, boiled or made into an omelette; cheese can be eaten in sandwiches, salads or in hot meals; beans and lentils can be eaten hot or in salads. There are many different types of fish and meat and all sorts of ways to prepare them.

Page 22
Sarah is exercising her arms. Sophie is exercising her legs. Tom is exercising both his arms and legs, but mainly his legs.

Page 23
Sam and Nicole need to replace the water that they have lost in sweating and the energy that they have used up while playing outside.

Index

About this book

Ways into Science is designed to encourage children to begin to think about their everyday world in a scientific way, examining cause and effect through close observation, recording their results and discussing what they have seen. Here are some pointers to gain maximum use from **Keeping Healthy**.

• Working through this book will introduce the basic concepts of keeping healthy and also some of the language structures and vocabulary associated with it (for example comparatives such as clean and cleanest). This will prepare the child for more formal work later in the school curriculum.

• On pages 11, 15 and 21 the children are invited to predict the results of a particular action or test. Ensure that you discuss the reason for any answer they give in some depth before turning over the page.

• On pages 13, 17 and 25 the children are invited to use their general knowledge to make a prediction about keeping healthy.

• On page 10 it is important to emphasise the first sentence on this page that it is natural for different people to grow at different rates.

• On page 12 spend some time discussing the healthy meals and looking at alternatives to items that a child may not like.

• On page 13 ask the child how to improve each of the meals to make them more healthy.

• Page 18 provides an opportunity for children to provide anecdotes about losing their teeth and gaining new ones.

• On page 25 you may need to develop the topic with sensitivity depending on the circumstances of the children. The role of the adult should be emphasised.